VICTORIAN ENGINEER

Contents

Designed and produced by David Salariya

Edited by Vicki Power

First published in 1994 by
PAN MACMILLAN CHILDREN'S BOOKS
A division of Pan Macmillan Limited
Cavaye Place London SW10 9PG

ISBN 0-333-5944-52 (Macmillan hardback)
ISBN 0-330-3299-44 (Piccolo paperback)

A CIP catalogue record for this book is available from the British Library

Printed in Hong Kong

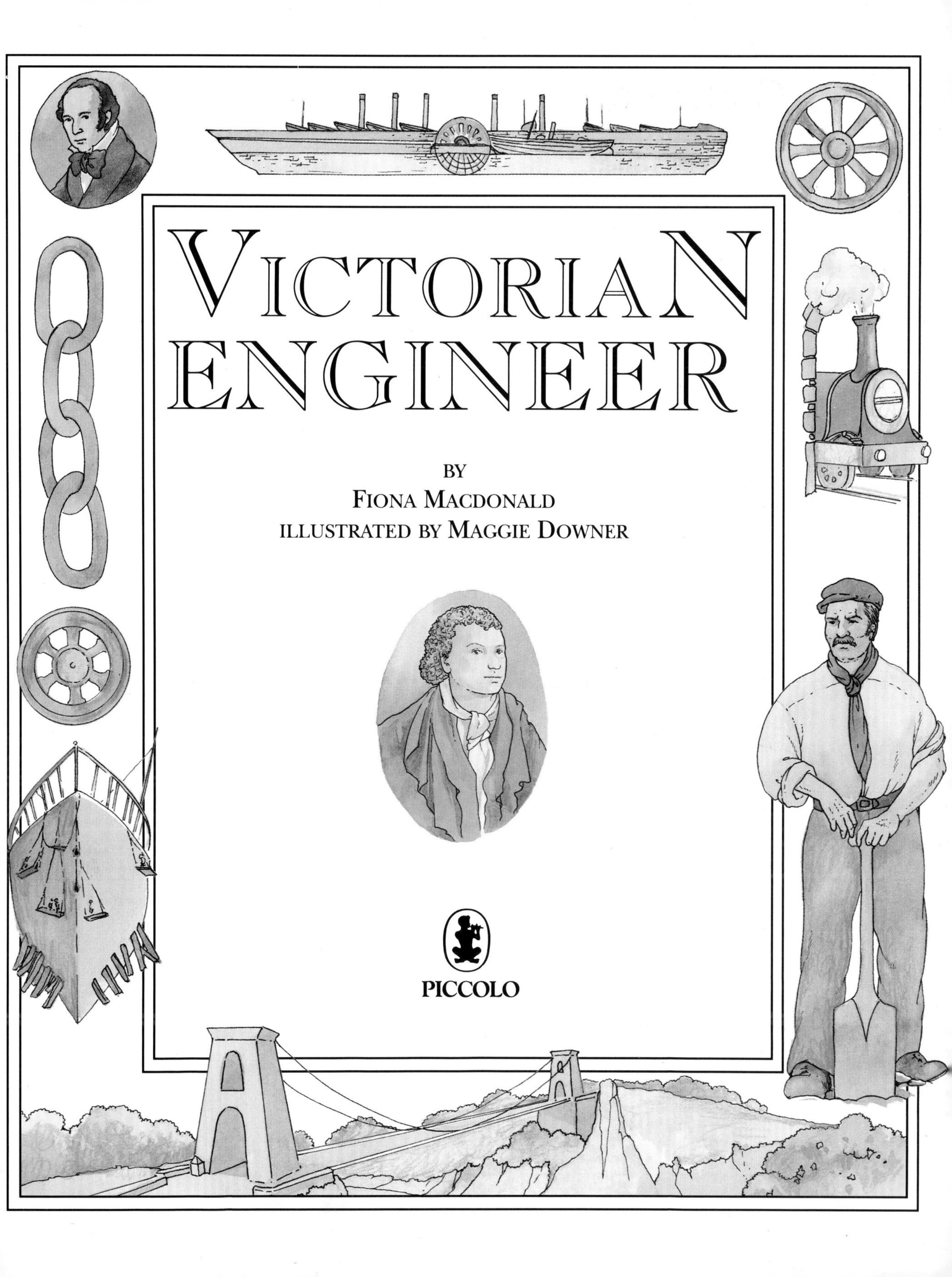

VICTORIAN ENGINEER

BY

FIONA MACDONALD

ILLUSTRATED BY MAGGIE DOWNER

PICCOLO

RAILWAYS
BUILT BY
1850
EDINBURGH
Glasgow
SCOTLAND
Hawick
Newcastle
Carlisle
Stockton
NORTH SEA
Workington
Darlington
Eastborough
Lancaster
York
IRISH
SEA
Leeds
Hull
Preston
Manchester
Holyhead
Liverpool
Sheffield
Lincoln
Chester
Crewe
Boston
Derby
Nottingham
Norwich
Birmingham
Peterborough
WALES
Cambridge
Ipswich
ENGLAND
Swansea
Swindon
LONDON
Chatham
Cardiff
Bristol
Canterbury
Dover
Barnstable
Southampton
Brighton
Hastings
Exeter
Weymouth
Plymouth
ENGLISH CHANNEL

Introduction

This book tells the story of one of the most famous nineteenth-century engineers: Isambard Kingdom Brunel. During his short but extremely active life (1806-1859), Brunel designed and built tunnels, bridges, railways and ships. He made vast sums of money, and then lost them again. He achieved glorious successes, and suffered tragic failures. When he died, people mourned him as 'England's greatest engineer . . . bold in his plans, but right.'

Brunel lived and worked at a time when England was changing very fast. Almost daily, it seemed, new machines were being invented, new factories were being built and new scientific discoveries were being made. Poor men and women left their homes in the country and moved to work in industrial cities. They hoped to get good wages and better jobs there. For Brunel, and for many other people who took part in this 'Industrial Revolution', life was tough, risky – and exciting.

THE INVENTOR'S FAMILY

Isambard Kingdom Brunel was born in Portsea, a busy town on the south coast of England. His father worked at the big navy dockyard there. The new baby got his unusual names from his parents. 'Isambard' (old-fashioned and French) was his father's middle name. 'Kingdom' was his mother's family name, before she married.

Sophia Kingdom, Isambard Brunel's mother. She married Marc Brunel in 1799. She supported him in all his work. Below: Marc Brunel (1769–1849), Isambard Brunel's father. Born in France, he came to live and work in England.

Isambard was the Brunels' third child, and their only son. Like his older sister, Sophie, he was bright and clever. Marc Brunel, their father, was an inventor and an engineer. He taught both of them to observe, to calculate and to draw. Soon, Isambard was sent away to boarding school. Later, he went to study technology with a famous firm of clock-makers in France.

Isambard's talent for engineering showed itself while he was still at school. He predicted that the wall of a new building nearby would not stay up, because it was so badly designed. He was right; it fell down.

Mass Production

Before the nineteenth century, goods were made by hand in small workshops or at home. There were few factories and few big machines. But now engineers were designing machines that could work faster than humans and turn out thousands of identical objects in a very short time. Marc Brunel was excited by all these new inventions and drew up plans for several machines. He discussed them with Henry Maudslay, owner of the best machine-making business in Britain.

Between 1803 and 1815 Britain was at war. Navy warships were powered by the wind. Their huge sails had to be raised and lowered by ropes which ran through pulleys. Millions of pulley-blocks were needed to help sailors with this task. Marc designed a machine to make blocks quickly and cheaply. Navy leaders were delighted. But peace was declared before Marc had time to sell his *next* mass-produced product. He was left with millions of pairs of machine-made army boots!

The machine for cutting wooden pulley-blocks designed by Marc Brunel and built by Henry Maudslay in 1803.

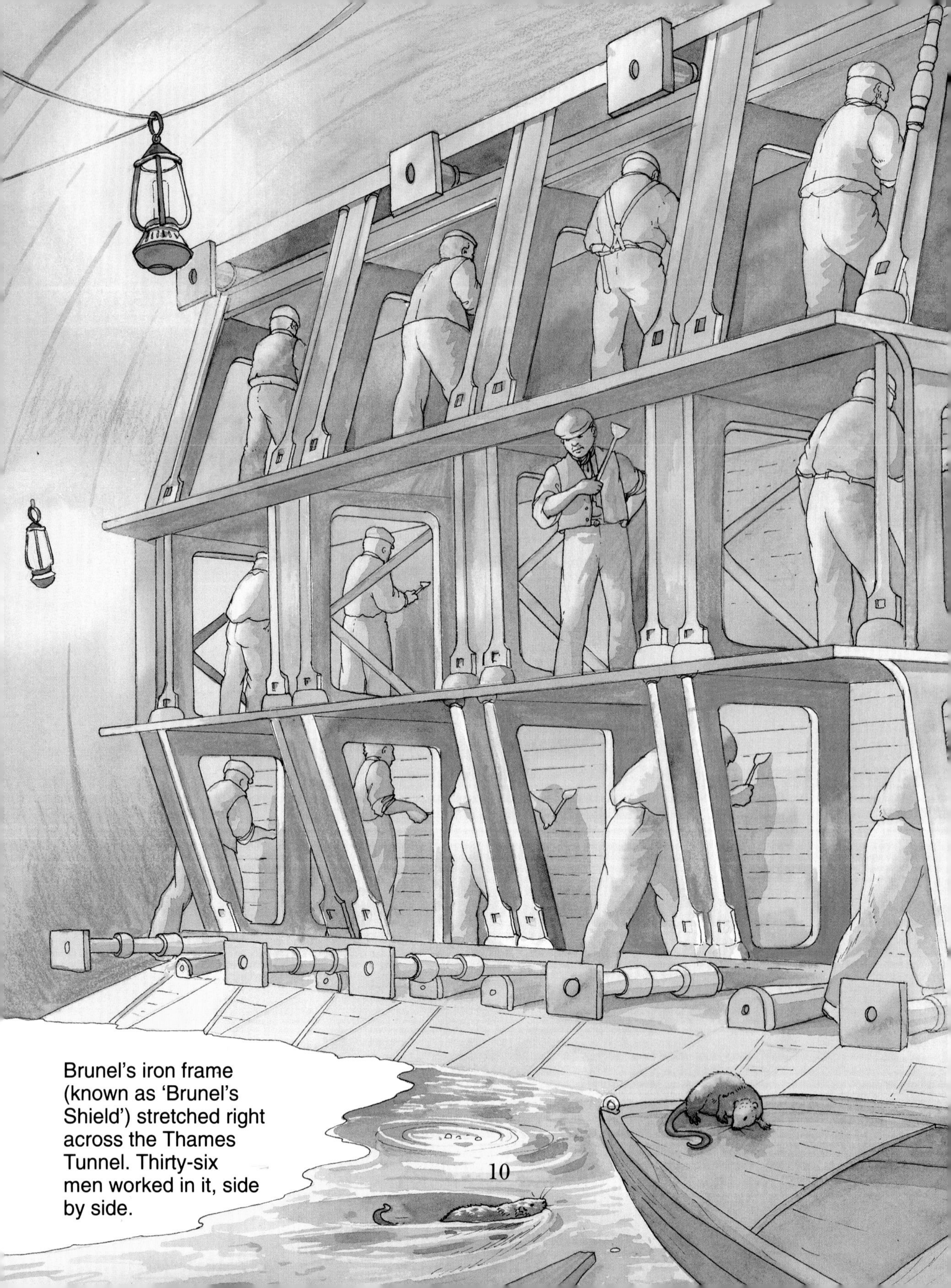

Brunel's iron frame (known as 'Brunel's Shield') stretched right across the Thames Tunnel. Thirty-six men worked in it, side by side.

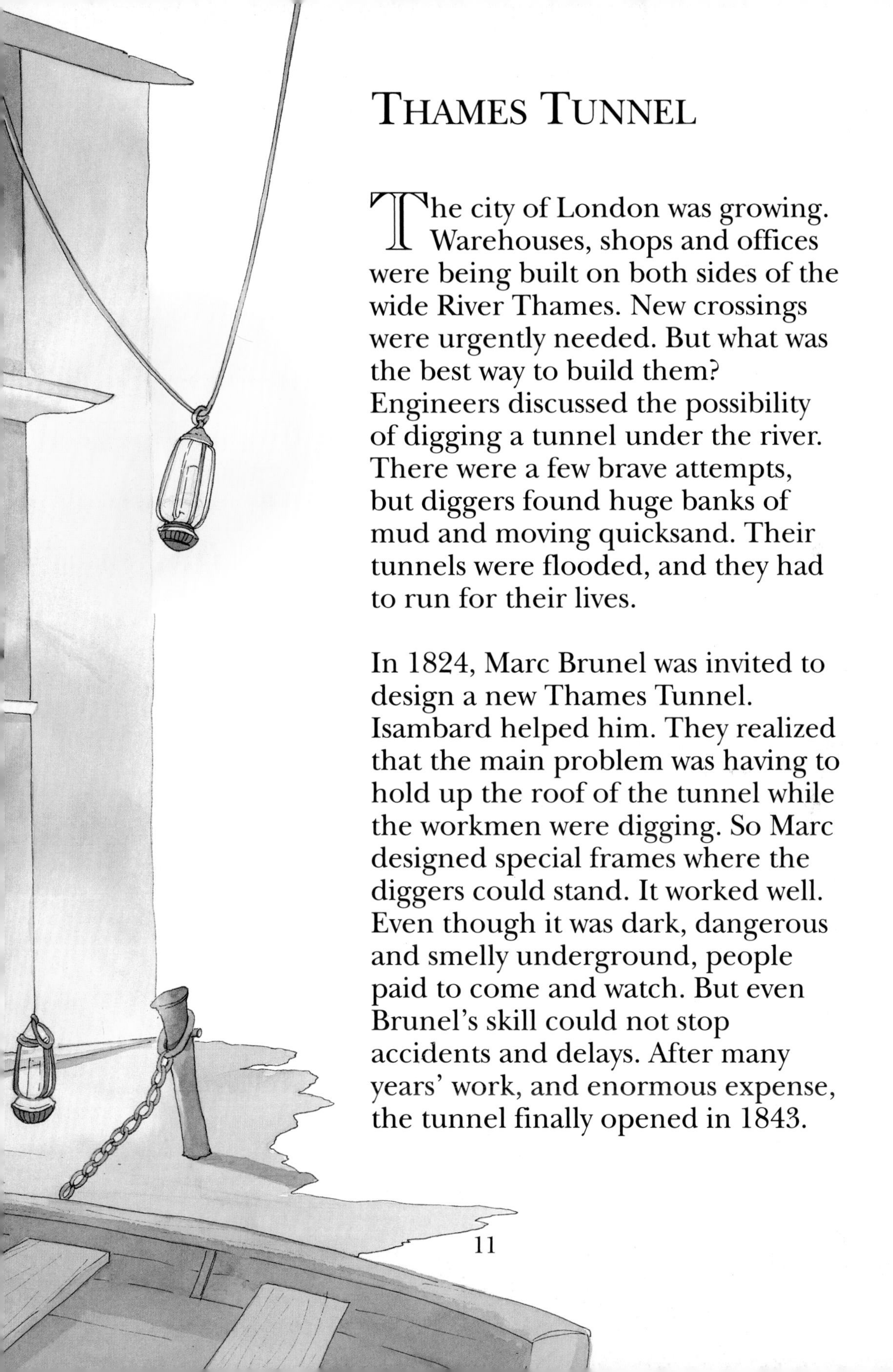

Thames Tunnel

The city of London was growing. Warehouses, shops and offices were being built on both sides of the wide River Thames. New crossings were urgently needed. But what was the best way to build them? Engineers discussed the possibility of digging a tunnel under the river. There were a few brave attempts, but diggers found huge banks of mud and moving quicksand. Their tunnels were flooded, and they had to run for their lives.

In 1824, Marc Brunel was invited to design a new Thames Tunnel. Isambard helped him. They realized that the main problem was having to hold up the roof of the tunnel while the workmen were digging. So Marc designed special frames where the diggers could stand. It worked well. Even though it was dark, dangerous and smelly underground, people paid to come and watch. But even Brunel's skill could not stop accidents and delays. After many years' work, and enormous expense, the tunnel finally opened in 1843.

Beautiful Bridges

Work on the Thames Tunnel was often delayed, by accidents and shortage of money. Marc Brunel was old and ill, and Isambard felt depressed. Would they ever succeed? But his doubts did not last long. He began to think of exciting new schemes. If tunnels were so difficult, why not build bridges, instead? Rich businessmen wanted big road bridges to carry goods to market. After 1825, railways needed bridges, too.

The completion of Brunel's last bridge, at Saltash, in Cornwall, was accompanied by great public celebrations. Queen Victoria's husband, Prince Albert, travelled by train from London to open it in May 1859.

In 1830, Isambard entered a competition to design a new bridge at Clifton, near Bristol. He did not win, but people were impressed by his ideas. Later, he went on to build some of the world's best bridges, using his engineering skills to work out ways of crossing very difficult sites. (After Brunel's death, a bridge was built at Clifton using his design.) His most famous bridge was the Royal Albert Bridge at Saltash, made of wrought iron. It spanned a valley 1,100 feet wide. It carried the first railway into Cornwall.

Home Sweet Home

In 1832, when he was twenty-five, Isambard Brunel met John Horsley, a composer and music teacher. Horsley was a friendly man, who had three lively, pretty daughters. They sketched and painted, sang and played the piano. Together, the Horsleys and their friends went for walks, or enjoyed long evenings. Young Brunel was romantic and impulsive. What could be better, he thought, after a day's work, than to relax in the company of such an interesting family?

Above: Isambard Brunel, from a portrait painted around 1833, when he was twenty-seven years old.
Below: Mary Horsley, his wife, from a portrait painted in 1831, when she was eighteen years old.

And so Brunel fell in love. In 1836, he married Mary, John Horsley's eldest daughter. She was very beautiful. They found a smart house in London, where Mary's elegant manners earned her the nickname of 'Duchess'. The Brunels had three children: Isambard, Henry Marc – who grew up to be another engineer – and Florence. They were happy, even though Isambard spent much of his time away from home, building new projects. As he wrote in his diary, he was, in some ways, 'married to his work'.

BUILDING THE RAILWAY

Millions of tons of earth had to be dug away by hand to make 'cuttings' through hillsides, so that railway tracks could be laid on flat, level ground. Where hills were made of solid rock, cuttings and tunnels were blasted out, using gunpowder.

The first regular railway service in Britain began in 1825. In the years that followed, many new companies were set up to build railways all over the country. To do this job they needed engineers.

In 1832, a group of Bristol merchants decided to try and build a railway from their home town to London. They had seen Brunel's

drawings for the Clifton bridge, and remembered him. In 1833, they asked him to survey the land where the railway track would run. For years, he travelled up and down, making plans and writing reports. He lived and worked in a specially converted horse-drawn carriage. Because it was large and black, it was called the 'Flying Hearse'.

This survey marked the start of one of Brunel's greatest achievements, the Great Western Railway. It was magnificently engineered. Even today, trains still use the London–Bristol route Brunel designed.

Railway Towns

Railways were built by manpower. Thousands of workmen used picks and shovels to construct a strong level 'bed' where the railway could be laid. They slept rough, in tents pitched beside the tracks. But once the railway was finished, new towns were built, close to railway stations, to house all the railway workers and their families.

It took a lot of people to run a railway. There were train drivers, firemen and guards. There were ticket collectors, porters, cleaners, signalmen, goods handlers and railway police. There were station caterers, newspaper sellers and cloakroom attendants. There were maintenance engineers, who repaired the trains and the tracks. They all needed somewhere to live.

Senior staff had spacious garden villas, in tree-lined streets. Ordinary workers lived in close-packed terraces. They joked, 'Nothing grows in our back yards, except children and washing.'

Sleepy, traditional market towns like Swindon (above) were transformed when railways were built. The new houses (right) were built of factory-made brick and slate, transported on railway wagons.

Travel for All

For over twenty years, Isambard Brunel built railways; 1,046 miles in all. Somehow he found time to experiment, as well. He designed 'atmospheric traction', with carriages driven by air. He chose new types of engines to pull his trains. He built extra-wide track for the Great Western Railway. All these were revolutionary ideas. But, while Brunel was working, another revolution was taking place. People were now travelling much farther than they had ever done before.

Railways brought travel for all. There were at least three classes of tickets, so even ordinary people could afford the fare. They travelled for all kinds of reasons – to meet business colleagues, to visit relatives, to go sight-seeing or just for fun. Railways also carried manufactured goods from big industrial cities to the ports, and brought fresh foods – like milk and vegetables – from the countryside, to feed people living in towns.

'All human life is here.' The platforms of nineteenth-century railway stations were crowded with all kinds of people: passengers, railway officials, food-sellers, beggars and thieves.

TRIUMPH AND DISASTER

Railways were not the only new form of transport in the nineteenth century. Ships, like trains, were now being powered by steam. In 1835, Brunel suggested that the Great Western Railway start a steamship service to New York.

People thought he was joking. But Brunel soon produced designs for a ship – *Great Western* – with a strong,

Great Britain, at Dundrum Bay, off the coast of Ireland in 1846. Brunel gave orders that its iron hull should be surrounded by thick padding, made of wood and straw, to protect it from winter storms.

stormproof hull that could carry enough fuel for the long voyage. He also installed powerful new engines. *Great Western* was launched in 1837, and received a triumphant welcome after crossing to New York. But Brunel was not satisfied. He was already planning another ship, to be made of iron.

This new steamship, *Great Britain*, made its first voyage in 1846. But it ran aground. Repairs cost a fortune. It was called 'a magnificent failure'.

The Great Ship

After 1851, Brunel devoted himself to only one project: designing a 'great ship' to sail non-stop to Australia. He reckoned that it would have to be six times larger than any ship built before. Brunel was not the sort of man to be frightened by this challenge. Instead, it fascinated him. In 1854, he began work on the *Great Eastern*. It was made of iron, with two different types of engines, and watertight compartments inside a double hull. It was 680 feet long, 83 feet wide and 58 feet high.

There were problems – with money, with colleagues, and with the ship itself. How could anything so big be moved from the dock where it was built? It was finally launched in 1858. But by now Brunel was a dying man, exhausted by over-work and disease. He lived to see his 'great ship' afloat, but never sailed in it. When a tragic accident almost wrecked it on its first sea voyage, the news was too much for him to bear. He died, just fifty-three years old.

Enormous chains were fastened to the hull of *Great Eastern*, to hold the ship back when it was launched. Brunel feared that unless its speed was slowed down, it would enter the water too quickly, and overturn.

Time Chart

Brunel's Life

1806 Isambard Brunel born.

1824 Helps his father with Thames Tunnel design.

1830 Enters competition to design Clifton Suspension Bridge. Fails, but gets noticed by businessmen.

1833 Begins work on Great Western Railway; acts as surveyor, architect and engineer. Continues to design bridges as well.

1836 Marries Mary Horsley.

1838 Begins to design ship *Great Britain.*

1846 *Great Britain* runs aground.

1852 Begins work on last bridge, at Saltash.

1854 Begins to build ship *Great Eastern.*

1859 *Great Eastern* sails, but major accident on board soon after; many killed.

1859 Brunel dies at fifty-three.

Europe and Middle East

1808 Richard Trevithick builds first passenger railway in London.

1810 Nicolas Apert (France) preserves food by heat-treatment.

1812 Gas street lighting first used in London.

1814 George Stevenson (UK) invents steam locomotive.

1822 Charles Babbage (UK) invents calculating machine; computers develop from this.

1825 First regular railway service (Stockton–Darlington, UK).

1839 L. J. Daguerre (France) invents simple form of photography.

1851 Great International Exhibition of science and industry in London.

1859 Joseph Lenoir (Belgium) invents internal combustion engine, now used in cars.

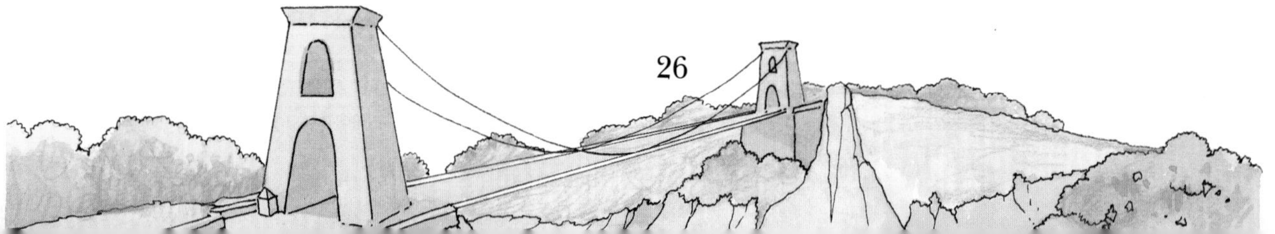

Asia and Africa

1815 Mount Tambora, a volcano in Indonesia, erupts; scientists discover that it has altered world climate for a year.

1829 Major new observatory, for studying the stars, built at Cape Town, South Africa.

1839 Nikolay Pzrhevalsky (Russia) leads scientific expedition to study wildlife of Central Asia.

1853 First railways and telegraph lines in India.

1858 Sir Jagadischandra Bose born in India. He is later famous for his scientific study of plants.

1858 Archaeologists de-code ancient Egyptian texts describing advanced mathematical ideas.

1859 Work starts on digging the Suez Canal (Egypt); when completed in 1869, it makes travel between Europe and the Far East quicker and cheaper.

North and South America

1807 Robert Fulton (USA) designs first workable steam-powered boat.

1809 First modern suspension bridge built in Massachusetts, USA.

1819 First steam-powered ship, *Savannah,* crosses the Atlantic Ocean.

1822 First 'scientific' investigation of Aztec remains in Mexico.

1829 W. Burt invents typewriter.

1834 C. H. McCormick patents machine to harvest corn.

1837 Samuel Morse invents Morse Code signals.

1841 James Eads invents diving bell (machine).

1851 Isaac Singer invents sewing machine.

1854 First elevator ('lift') built in New York.

1859 First oil well drilled in Pennsylvania.

Word List

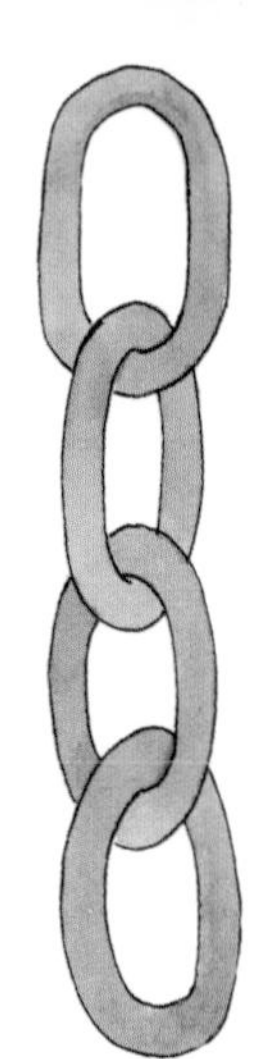

Aground When a ship is washed ashore, usually by high winds or stormy weather.

Archaeology The study of people and cultures of the past, by examining their remains.

'Atmospheric traction' One of Isambard Brunel's inventions. Railway wagons and carriages were driven along by air pressure. It was never fully developed.

Calculate To work out sums or number problems.

Caterers People who prepare and sell ready-to-eat food.

Colleagues Work-mates.

Compartments Sections.

Convert To change something so that it can be used in another way.

Cuttings 'Passageways' cut through hillsides so that a level track can be made where trains can run.

Diving bell An early type of submarine.

Dockyard A place with docks and workshops where ships and boats are built and repaired.

Engineer Someone who has studied the science of making, building and maintaining things. Today, people who design bridges and railways, like Brunel did, are called civil engineers. Other types of engineers include mechanical engineers (cars and machines), aeronautical engineers (aircraft), chemical engineers (chemical machinery) and electrical engineers (communications systems and electrical machinery).

Factory A place where things are made by machines.

Fare The money paid by passengers to travel on a bus, train, ferry, taxi, etc.

Fireman (on railways) Someone whose job it was to keep the fires burning steadily under railway engine boilers. These boilers heated water to produce the steam which powered the train.

Hearse A large carriage or car used to carry a dead body on the way to a funeral. Almost always painted black.

Hull The part of a ship which 'sits' in the water.

Identical Exactly the same.

Impulsive Acting quickly, without always stopping to think about what might happen next.

Isolated Alone; by itself.

Maintenance Looking after.

Manufactured Made, usually by machine.

Mass-produced Made in large quantities, usually by machines in factories.

Mourn To feel sad when someone dies.

Observe To look at very closely, and (often) make a note of what you see.

Pick A heavy tool, like a spike on the end of a long handle, used to dig up the ground.

Porter A person whose job is to carry luggage and parcels at a railway station or hotel.

Predicted Forecast; said in advance what would happen.

Pulley-blocks Carefully shaped pieces of wood, with grooves where ropes can run smoothly. Used to haul heavy loads to a great height.

Pulleys A system of ropes and pulley-blocks used to haul heavy loads to a great height.

Quicksand Patches of ground where sand is mixed with water to form a sticky mass. If you tread in a quicksand, you are sucked into it, sink, and can drown.

Remote A long way away.

Revolution A drastic change in the way things are done. Commonly used to describe the overthrow of a government.

Shovel A tool like a spade, used for digging the ground.

Site The place where something is built.

Sketched Made quick, attractive drawings.

Slate A type of rock that can be split neatly into thin sheets. These are then used to cover roofs.

Spacious With plenty of room.

Survey (in engineering) To make a detailed map by calculating and measuring distances and height.

Suspension bridge A bridge that hangs from cables or chains that are connected to towers at each end.

Terraces Rows of houses, built so each house is joined on to the one next door.

Transformed Completely changed.

Wages Payment for work.

Warehouse A place where goods are stored.

Wrought iron A type of iron (a metal used in building) specially produced to be tough and very long lasting.

INDEX

NOTE: Page numbers in bold refer to illustrations.

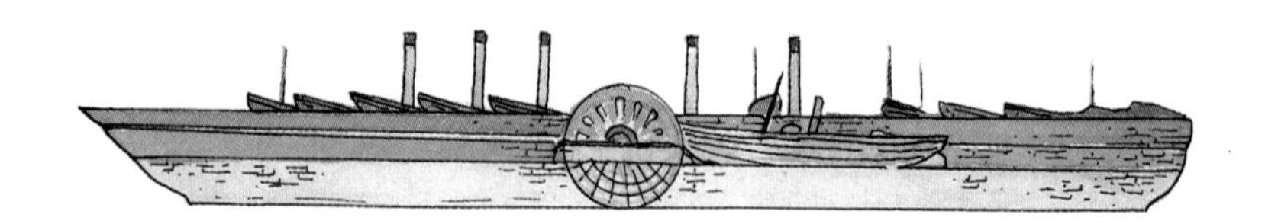

Notes for Teachers on History in the National Curriculum

The new National Curriculum for History, which lays down a prescribed course of study for pupils aged five to sixteen, was introduced into schools in England and Wales during the autumn term 1991.

This series of books has been designed to provide background information relevant to the designated Core History Study Units for key Stage 2 (i.e., for pupils aged seven to eleven), and also to the Optional History Study Units at the same key stage level. Younger children, in particular, should find the short, simple text and largely visual presentation of information appropriate to their needs.

Victorian Engineer relates in particular to Core Study Unit CSU 3 – Victorian Britain. In the words of the National Curriculum final programme of study (*History in the National Curriculum*, HMSO, March 1991, page 23):

> Pupils should be introduced to life in Victorian Britain and its legacy to the present day. The focus should be on men, women and children at different levels of society, in different areas of Victorian England, Wales, Scotland and Ireland, and how they were affected by industrialization.
>
> Pupils should be taught about:
>
> economic developments: steam power, industry and mass production . . .
> new forms of transport, including railways
>
> the growth of towns...
>
> scientific and cultural achievements: inventions and scientific discoveries
> buildings and public works . . .

All these topics are included in this book.

RAILWAYS BUILT BY 1850
EDINBURGH
Glasgow
SCOTLAND
Hawick
Newcastle
Carlisle
Workington
Darlington
Stockton
NORTH SEA
Eastborough
Lancaster
York
Leeds
Hull
Preston
IRISH SEA
Holyhead
Liverpool
Manchester
Sheffield
Lincoln
Chester
Crewe
Boston
Derby
Nottingham
Norwich
Birmingham
Peterborough
WALES
Cambridge
Ipswich
ENGLAND
Swansea
Swindon
LONDON
Chatham
Cardiff
Bristol
Canterbury
Barnstable
Dover
Southampton
Brighton
Hastings
Exeter
Weymouth
Plymouth
ENGLISH CHANNEL